There Will Be A Fulfillment

Hear It * See It * Believe It * Say It * Receive It

Blessed is she who believed, for there will be a fulfillment of those things which were told her from the Lord." Luke 1:45 NKJV

Karen Seymore Portman

Dedication

If the vision for you, a family member, a friend, a co-worker, or anyone you know has been distorted or blinded, then this book is for you.

This book is dedicated to all those who dare to dream again. As you turn the pages, you'll be unlocking your destiny.

Table of Contents

INTRODUCTION

I pray that you will allow this book to take you on a spiritual journey so that anything blocking your vision will be removed and you will propel forward into your God-given destiny.

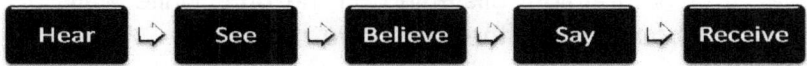

Hear	⇨	See	⇨	Believe	⇨	Say	⇨	Receive

Let the Lord be the light that guides your vision. I want that for myself, and I want it for you too!

Blessings,

Karen Seymore Portman

Chapter 1
THE DREAM

In the early fall of 2011, I had a dream about my deceased paternal grandmother. She was living in a large, absolutely beautiful two-level home. Each room was fully and finely decorated with crown molding lining the walls. The foyer was very spacious, about the size of a large sitting area, with a lot of natural light glistening off the pure white walls and almost bouncing off the expensive chandelier. The shiny dark hardwood floors in the foyer matched the staircase leading to the upper level. The railing along the staircase was a bright, sparkling white with not a dust particle in sight. Every room was spacious. Although this was my grandmother's house in the dream, everything was quite different from where she lived before she passed.

Perhaps I should clarify. Where she lived in the natural was a very nice community, primarily for senior living even though it was not an area set aside only for seniors. Just to give you a mental image of her actual dwelling, she was blessed with a one level, four bedroom home in a quiet neighborhood. That was unheard of for a single senior woman on a fixed income in the deep south of the Carolina's. It was considered the "senior projects" by locals because most of the occupants were seniors living on a fixed income; therefore, it was considered normal living arrangements. Although Grandma certainly had a lot of space then, this dream was telling another story.

Grandma was hosting some type of family social. Relatives from several generations were there, including members from my maternal side of the family, which was unusual.

Both sides of my family rarely, if ever, socialized together at joint gatherings. It's not an overstatement to say Grandma's house was chocked-full of relatives upon relatives.

In the dream I was staying in a room located on the far side of the house – in another wing – to help you visualize the size of this home. I was in the middle of dressing for the family social when I heard the doorbell ringing. Whoever was at the door kept ringing the bell continuously with only a slight pause between each ring to allow time for someone to answer, but no one did. It was obvious the visitor was not giving up because the ringing continued.

Because I was on the far side of the house, I remember thinking, "With a house full of people, why isn't anyone answering the door?" I thought someone would eventually answer so I waited. After I don't know how many rings, I headed down the long hallway and down the stairs towards the door. Wouldn't you know it? Just as I was approaching the door, so was my grandmother.

Now picture this next scene in slow motion because it was all happening simultaneously. As she was reaching towards the doorknob, I was looking at her very strangely, as if in a daze. Although she looked like herself, the way I remember Grandma, something seemed different. Her features were the same. Her "around the house" dress was the same. So that wasn't it. It was something else, but I couldn't quite put my finger on it. Then, I gazed into her eyes and said to myself, "It looks like her vision is off." It was at that time that her hand touched the doorknob, and she opened the door.

A uniformed repairman was standing there, his name embroidered on the shirt, and a tool box in his hand. It was obvious he had come to fix something. It also was obvious he had been there many times before because of the way he and Grandma greeted each other. He gave her a warm, friendly greeting, "Hello, Miss Rose" (fictitious), like most people who knew her did. And just like I remember Grandma, with a slight stutter, she warmly returned the greeting.

With my mouth still wide open, the repairman walked past me, saying, "Hello," immediately followed by, "you know she's blind, right?"

Whoa! That shocked me. I passionately replied, "No, I didn't." The repairman continued, "Oh yes, she's blind and has been like that for years. She can't see a thing!" Then he left me standing there with my mouth open and eyes bulging. I suppose he went on to take care of what he came to repair because I never saw him again.

With my mouth still open and eyes fixed on Grandma as she was making her way back to the kitchen, I confronted her about her sight. I needed to know if it was true; and if so, why hadn't she told anyone. Why didn't we see it before? Anxiously awaiting an answer, I kept following her. At this point, my questions outnumbered her answers.

Finally, to my surprise and probably because I refused to go away, Grandma responded, "Yes, I am blind, and I've been meaning to go to the doctor but just haven't. I'll go one day." After that, she entered the kitchen to begin preparing dinner. I guess that meant our conversation was over on the issue of Grandma's eyesight.

I watched her move around the kitchen preparing for this family event. Grandma didn't miss a beat doing anything. A little flour here, a little flour there; a little spice here, a little spice there. She continued to move around the kitchen, firing up the stove as if everything was normal. Every burner was ablaze with huge flames covering the entire bottom of the pots and rising a little along the sides. The large cast iron pots and pans emitted steam like a large steamboat. Grandma was busy preparing for the gathering, bustling around the kitchen, cooking dishes to perfection, without measuring any ingredients!

I watched in silence but my mind was still going back to the words spoken by the repairman and the confirmation from my grandmother. She continued cooking and handling the chores as usual. She knew where everything was located and put just the right amount of ingredients in each dish she was preparing. It was just another normal day in the life of Grandma, that is, until the scene changed to the family dinner around the table.

All the generations from both sides of my paternal and maternal families were seated around a very large round banquet table. Grandma stood off a slight distance, ensuring everyone had what they needed. After all, this is what grandmothers do, right? I was waiting for Grandma to tell the family something about her vision since I had asked earlier, but she didn't. I thought surely someone else will notice and say something, but they didn't. She moved around the table like a server, helping people pass the bowls and plates as if nothing was wrong. And to her, it wasn't.

Grandma fixed a plate for my dad; however, by the time it reached him, it had gotten cold. Dad pushed it back and folded his arms. Sounding and acting like a seven year old, dad said he didn't want it. He became more irritated because no one was moved by his tantrum, especially one of my sisters. I guess he couldn't understand how everyone could be laughing, eating, and having a good time when he was not happy because his food was served (or had gotten) cold. Dad pouted throughout the entire dinner. It appeared everyone at the dinner thought this was just a normal family gathering where a little drama is always present.

Although Grandma appeared to be hurt by my dad's behavior, she never said anything. As for me, I was still shocked looking at everyone 'just functioning' in this abnormality and not saying a word about my grandmother's condition, or the commotion around the table. I thought, "Can't they see what's going on?" I was still waiting for Grandma to tell the family about her vision, but she didn't.

Then, I woke up.

CHAPTER 2
MY INTERPRETATION AND THE TRUTH REVEALED

Although the characters in the dream were family members, I believe the dream also was for the Body of Christ. The family members were in it so I could recognize, by the people, what was normal, what was out of character, and looking from a different place now, what needed to be changed that had been accepted as normal for years.

> *And you shall know the truth, and the truth shall make you free. John 8:32*

Regardless of whether we recognize it or admit it, all families have some type of drama, secrets, or dysfunctional behavior going on at times. However, I believe this dream was meant for me to see light coming into chaos treated as normal so families and others could be set free.

I penned the dream in my journal. Over time, the Holy Spirit began revealing the meaning to me. What I found very interesting is, when I penned the dream in my journal, the first time I wrote "repairman," I used a lower case "r". However, the second time I wrote it, I used an uppercase "R". I was not aware of this difference until I read it later. Could the Repairman have been the Deliverer (the Savior) coming to bring sight to the blind? *Pause and think about that.*

Once the Deliverer shows up, truth is revealed. Once the Deliverer shows up, dysfunctional behavior is brought to light so generational bondages that have held captives imprisoned are broken. I believe this was a dream for everyone with ears to hear.

Here are some key pointers the Lord revealed to me immediately after the dream:

- My grandmother's appearance was the same as I remembered her when she was alive. Therefore, at a glance in the dream, Grandma appeared normal because of the way she was moving around, handling the day-to-day chores, cooking without ever missing a beat, and all the other things sighted grandmas do. I guess that's why no one ever noticed anything was 'off' and, therefore, never said anything to her.

- My grandmother obviously knew about her loss of sight but accepted it as normal. Therefore, she adapted to her environment and tried to fool others around her, including herself. Masking problems is a way of not acknowledging that they exist. If we remain in a situation long enough, we, too, can accept the condition as normal; thereby, remaining spiritually blind ... just functioning. We accept the lie and adapt the fantasy to our environment.

- My grandmother's home was well-lit with beautiful furnishings. Everything looked impeccable on the outside; yet she was dealing with a spiritual handicap. This disguise may be true for some of us. I believe this portion of the dream was used to speak to our spiritual house -- our temple (the body). We dress up and adorn our mess with things so that the outward appearance will fool some; however, we can't fool God. Once His light shines in our darkness, someone will notice. The bell will ring!

- The house was full of other family members, but no one else heard the *repairman* ringing the doorbell. With that said, although I didn't see this in the dream, my family probably didn't notice the repairman was in the house either. Or if they did, perhaps they didn't think it was odd to have someone there to repair something. It was just another ordinary day. But with persistency, he kept ringing the bell trying to get someone's attention that *something needed attention.* Until it's noticed and fixed, those things will continue to affect all future generations. I believe the repairman's persistence was symbolic of Jesus' knocking, trying to get the attention of at least one with ears to hear the *Deliverer* at the door or perhaps even answering prayers of days gone by from other loved ones!

- Representatives from all generations were present, but no one seemed to notice the dysfunctional behavior. Or perhaps they did but didn't want to say anything. After all, who wants to rock the boat at a family gathering if everything is going "as normal". But I believe God is looking for someone with spiritual eyes to stir the water in order to bring healing to present and future generations. Otherwise, if not corrected, dysfunctional behavior will continue to be accepted as the norm and pass from one generation to another, accepted as the norm, until at least one notices and speaks up.

- The repairman confirmed what I was thinking about my grandmother's vision being off when I met them at the door. In fact, he didn't say that her vision was off. He said she was blind and had been that way for a long time. Therefore, what I was sensing and seeing was correct when I saw her. I believe that was an indication that God will open someone's eyes to see abnormalities in order to bring healing to situations – especially families.

- My father got so upset that no one cared about his food being served cold, and no one offered to warm it. This sulking could have several meanings, including uncovering relationship issues between a mother and son; the lack of concern we display when someone is upset; or another dysfunction that is yet to be unraveled.

I am sure pieces of this dream will continue to unfold over time. However, after pondering over this dream a few months later, I was reminded of the story of the man healed at the pool of Bethesda after an encounter with Jesus in Mark 5:1-15. The text says this man had a condition for 38 years and was waiting for someone to put him in the water when it stirred. Jesus knew he had been in that condition for a long time; and just like my grandmother in the dream, the passage in Mark 5 represents so many of us. We say we've been meaning to get help or hoping someone will help us; but until then, we keep functioning in our comfort zone or dazing in our den of denial. I wonder why that is? Could it be because we never cry out for the Deliverer to help us?

If we don't seek help from our Deliverer, the end result will be that we remain spiritually handicapped and exist by learning to function instead of truly living. And just like my father in the dream, we will look at our life as if we've been served a cold plate of indifference by people who are supposed to love us.

Or perhaps pushing the plate away could represent rejecting help from those God placed around us because it's not what we're accustomed to or from a source we expected to receive it. Therefore, we remain upset and filled with other negative emotions as we watch others "feast" and enjoy the celebration (or gathering).

Even more so, perhaps instead of waiting for someone to fix it for us, we need to ask God and co-labor with Him and get up to do something for ourselves. Maybe the food could represent God's manna so it's either feast or famine on His Word, but we have to decide!

But here is another sad thought. The dream could have represented yet another family gathering where everyone is together smiling; but behind all the laughter, the gathering is flooded with tears. Tears from unresolved issues that have gone unnoticed or unaddressed over the years, and no one dares to upset the status quo. The dream could represent so many of us who are so blinded by circumstances that we cannot see the vision God really has for us; therefore, we miss the rapture of too many divine destinies. Has our love grown cold to the Server that we're pushing Him away to another day, another season, or for some other reason?

God wants our vision restored so we can move forward into our divine destiny; however, there are some steps we must take to get there. Living involves transformation that brings change. But in order to start the process, we must hear it, see it, believe it, say it, and receive it. It's just that simple. Our mouth, our ego, and our actions must come into agreement with what we believe in our heart so we can receive God's promises with wide, open arms.

Again, more revelation is bound to come about this dream, but one thing is abundantly clear. If we continue walking around spiritually blind, we will not hear the Deliverer knocking at the door. Our blinded state will cause us to miss out on too many blessings until we make the decision to remove the blinders and get the necessary help. Lost vision is lost destiny.

As we head on this spiritual journey, I would encourage you to read Luke 1:26-56 in a couple of different versions; I will reference the reading in the Message Bible frequently. I absolutely love the way it tells the story of Mary's visitation, her acceptance, and her cousin's reaction. The first time I read it in this version I could feel the words coming to life; quickening me like fire in my spirit. It felt as if I was there -- right there in the moment. As I was reading it, I also saw several things happening, which ties into our own **hear-see-believe-say-receive** journey so we can move forward. Therefore, come with me to explore this idea further.

Chapter 3
HEAR IT: DID WE HEAR WHAT GOD SAID?

The visitation Mary received from Gabriel, the messenger angel, spoke a word into her hearing. I'm sure the visitation alone caught Mary off guard; but even more so, I'm sure what Gabriel had to say was not what she was expecting (Luke 1:30-35). The words spoken to her forever changed any image she probably had of herself or what she perceived others thought about her. After all, how could someone who was possibly considered to be so insignificant be handpicked for something so significant? Mary heard these words from Gabriel. If she had any doubts, they were removed. Gabriel's message to Mary caused her to see herself the way God saw her and refocus her vision so she could see her assignment as God's handmaiden.

> *In the sixth month of Elizabeth's pregnancy, God sent the angel Gabriel to the Galilean village of Nazareth to a virgin engaged to be married to a man descended from David. His name was Joseph, and the virgin's name, Mary. Luke 1:26-27*

But let's back up one step. In order for Mary to be able to hear from God's messenger, she had to be in position for the visitation. Even more so, in order for Mary to recognize the message was from God, she had to be in relationship with Him. This condition is critical.

In Mary's ear-gate (her hearing), the angel spoke to her

identity just the way God saw her. Depending on which Bible version you are reading, the angel used words like, beautiful, highly favored, and chosen by God. Selah. Just pause and think about that for a moment. Then, he spoke to her purpose. Mary was chosen by God to carry the Promise (Jesus). If there was any fear in her mind, the angel assured her not to be afraid because it was of God. The angel spoke to Mary's fear, and she had to hear it.

God speaks to all of us in so many ways but we have to be listening to hear His voice as well as positioned. It's easy to get caught up in the daily cares of life and forget things He's told us to do. I would imagine that we make a note somewhere, probably using some form of technology or the old fashioned way – pen and ink. But, if you're like me, it's easy to get caught up doing "stuff" and forget to go back to the notes.

Therefore, periodically, I take time to revisit words spoken to me from the Lord. I'm often amazed at what I've forgotten. I'm even more amazed and sorry when I realize I missed a deadline or that one thing I haven't done that was clearly a missing link in order to get to the next thing. Why? All because I simply forgot. When that happens, I quickly repent so I can move forward.

So has God spoken anything to you? Have you had a surprise visitation from Him? If so, what did He say? What have you done with the information? To freely hear the Holy Spirit speaking, we cannot have selective hearing. In other words, we cannot choose to hear what we want to hear, and lower the volume on things that we don't want to hear because we simply don't want to do them. We have to be open to hear what the Spirit is saying so we can move to the next phase – to see it.

Chapter 4
SEE IT: CAN WE SEE WHAT GOD SAID?

Like Mary, we need a visitation from the Lord so we can hear what He has to say. Then after hearing, we need vision to

> *And Mary said, Yes, I see it all now:*
> *Luke 1:38a*

see it. We might have a question or two on the "how," and the explanation may not make any sense to us (if we get one at all); however, if we believe the Word of God, we're told that with God all things are possible if we only believe (Mark 9:23). Mary heard it and saw it. Like Mary, our vision can change about our current circumstances from a single visitation. Once the Spirit speaks life into a dead situation, things change if we can see it.

Close your eyes for a moment and use your imagination. Picture a visitation from the Lord however He chooses to send it. Get a picture in your mind about what He is saying. Just a brief moment like this can cause you to see way beyond your present situation. If you really see it, you'll begin to step out of your box of limitation and arise with Kingdom vision. After all, it is written that without vision God's people perish (Proverbs 29:18). When we lose our vision, we lose our hope.

When we can see what He's spoken in our hearing, we know we can have it. We may not have the steps to get there yet, but our focus will shift. We begin to see where He wants to take us. Our eyes will be opened to see the greatness, the potential, the depth, and the expansion that God purposed for us (Jeremiah 29:11). God knows how to gently correct our distorted blurry vision, and heal our blinded eyes by showing us the good things He has in store for us. Never mind what others may have said in the past. When God speaks, it is so. He watches over His word to perform it (Jeremiah 1:12). When God speaks, we need to see it and so it is.

Mary responded by saying, "Yes, I see it all now..." (The Message). Her sight changed; therefore, her perception changed. I say Mary now had a Kingdom vision. How Mary saw the situation was preparing her for the next steps she would have to take, including possible ridicule and rejection by others, perhaps starting with her betrothed husband.

This is very important for us as we travel along this spiritual journey on the way to our next destination. When we begin to see things the way God sees them, it will realign our thoughts with His. After all, God's thoughts are higher than ours, and the way He would go about it is not like our ways (Isaiah 55:8-9). This would definitely raise our level of expectation to see from a different point of view. We have to get imaginative with it because we serve a creative God.

To illustrate an example of seeing what you know you "heard," several years ago, when my son was around eight years of age (he's grown now), we were having Friday Family Night. This was a time we would either go out to eat or order in and watch movies or play a game. One night we decided to play *The Game of Life* (also known as *LIFE*), a board game by the Milton Bradley Company.

For those of you who are unfamiliar with this game, this is where you travel around the board by spinning the wheel and going the number of spaces shown on the dial. Each person would follow the directions on the landed board space or by following the directions on a card drawn. Players would eventually choose a career, spouse, number of children, their house, and make other decisions along the way by following the directions given.

By "luck of the draw," my son chose the career of a doctor with a six-figure income. He was elated. After all, even at age eight, he knew that a doctor was a lucrative career – at least in most cases. He continued around the board – picked up a wife and some children along the way before he had to pull another card to choose his house. The card he pulled from the deck, again by "luck of the draw," was a real fixer-upper, a handyman special. The house had steps caved in, a deteriorated roof, fallen or missing siding, and many other dilapidated, unattractive conditions. It appeared uninhabitable, one that garnered few if any sellers. The price tag on it was cheap, but it was no deal to him.

My son was never one, at this time in life, who could hide his emotions. So I watched his countenance completely change. I laughed. So out of the mouth of this eight year old, he exclaimed, "This is not the way a doctor is supposed to live!" I laughed hysterically, but he found absolutely no humor in it. His face remained serious and stern. Yes, even at eight years of age, he knew what he "saw" on the card was not what he "heard" in terms of how a doctor should be living. Because of what he *heard*, he could not *see* anything differently. Therefore, very quietly, he proceeded to put the card back in the deck.

Still laughing, probably with tears rolling down at this point, I corrected him. "You can't put that back. It's cheating!" So honoring what I said, he didn't put it back. Instead, he simply crumpled it up, tossed it to the side on the floor out of reach, and just drew another card. I guess that was his way of making a statement that not only was he not going to keep the card but he didn't want anyone else to get it. Either it would be removed totally or instantly recognizable. The card was now marked ... forever!

The point of the story: at eight years old my son had a vision based on something he heard in the natural. He threw the card aside because he knew that somehow what he saw did not match what he was told (or thought) doctors could afford. The vision did not line up.

Sometimes we have cards we need to toss out of our deck (sight) so we can see the God-vision. We need to toss some cards out of our deck (sight) so that generations will no longer focus on the old, but they will be blessed with the new vision we put in place. I guess another way of seeing this is: it doesn't matter what hand life has dealt us, with Kingdom mentality our vision can change and affect others with whom we come into contact. Then, just like Mary, our current status will no longer matter. The only thing that will matter is the new vision that God has shared with us. We should then be able to get on board with His plan for our lives and follow Him.

Imagine it. When God speaks to us, we hear it and get a mental picture of the manifestation of His Word. When we hear His voice of guidance, promise, instruction, or the like, we should visualize it, which transforms the impossibility to attainability. We then believe God and not others for our new image. This process brings us to the next step – believe.

Chapter 5
BELIEVE IT: DO WE BELIEVE WHAT GOD SAID?

Mary heard, saw, and now believed. When she accepted God's design for her life, she got on board with God's plan.

> *I'm the Lord's maid, ready to serve. Let it be with me just as you say. Then the angel left her.*
> *Luke 1:38b*

Who's to say that Mary didn't question the roadmap ahead? We don't know, but the key here is in her response, *"I'm the Lord's maid, ready to serve. Let it be with me just as you say."*

Mary came into agreement. Her cousin Elizabeth could feel and see it when Mary came to visit her. Elizabeth, also expecting a child at the time, said the baby in her womb leaped. She knew Mary believed because she said, *"Blessed is she who <u>believed</u>, for there will be a fulfillment of those things which were told her from the Lord." (Luke 1:45 NKJV).*

To be in agreement, Mary had to believe in her heart what was spoken and what she saw. She had to accept it intellectually first. Her way of thinking had to change (the mind). She had to be willing to do what her Lord would have her to do even if it meant ridicule or changing directions. This new thing happening in her life, although a great honor, it could cause her to suffer before the blessing manifests.

She would have to walk through the shame and humiliation of being pregnant when she was supposed to be a virgin. She had to believe that Joseph would still want to marry her

25

once he found out. If not, she had to be willing to accept the consequences, even if it meant possibly losing him. She had to believe that what was spoken by Gabriel (the messenger angel) would truly come to pass even if others thought she was crazy.

Some may be familiar with the 1989 movie, *Field of Dreams*. In the movie, Ray, played by Kevin Costner, heard a "voice" speaking to him, giving him an action: "Build it and they will come." In order to "build it" (a baseball field), he had to plow his crop (his livelihood). In one scene, he's out there plowing up the crop and the townspeople are gathered – watching, laughing and talking amongst themselves. They were certain he had lost his mind. After all, his crop was his source of income.

But because he was sure he heard "the voice", against all odds, he did it. He ignored the ridicule and plowed the field. Then the winter came in more ways than one. Not only was it cold outside, but the bills were piling up and foreclosure of the farm was presented as an option. It was a painful process, filled with many decisions. However, one day, through a confirming dream given to the couple (what I call their visitation) it was evident that they were on the right path. The "voice" spoke again. They continued to follow the "voice" and waited for the full manifestation to happen. In the end, it all worked out, all because he was willing to follow, "the voice".

He kept saying what he heard to his family. As he followed, so did his family. I like to think of this as leading the generations too by plowing new ground. No pun intended. This leads to the next part, saying.

Chapter 6
SAY IT: WILL WE SAY WHAT GOD SAID?

Matthew 12:34b says, "For out of the abundance of our heart our mouth speaks." Mary believed in her heart the message that was delivered to her; therefore, she was able to burst forth in praise. Her praise filled the atmosphere around her.

> *And Mary said, I'm bursting with God-news; I'm dancing the song of my Savior God. God took **one good look at me**, and look what happened—I'm the most fortunate woman on earth! Luke 1:46-48a*

The Message Bible states it this way from Mary: "I'm bursting with God-news", as she quickly made her way to Elizabeth's house to share it. Although this was not Mary's case with Elizabeth, I would add a word of caution here. Everyone will not be excited to hear our "*God-news*" (as the Message Bible states it). Therefore, we need to make sure we're led by God before running to others to share what was revealed.

Excitement sprung from Mary's voice. Someone who could have been once viewed as no one significant was appreciative of the love her Lord had for her. A visitation from Gabriel, the messenger angel, changed her vision and now, she was able to dance. The message from the Lord marked a turning point in her life, and she came into agreement. In verse 48, some versions say, "From now on ..." or "For behold, henceforth all generations will call me blessed."

In other words, I believe Mary was saying, from this moment on things will never be the same in my life. Some of us probably need to say, "from this moment on" over some revelations from the Lord. From this moment on, I don't care what you thought about me, this is who I am now. From this moment on, the image I had of myself has changed. From this moment on, I heard it, I saw it, I believe it, and now I'm saying it. We can say from this moment on to whatever the change is that has taken place in our lives from a visit with a thankful heart.

It marked Mary's turning point; and it can mark ours, too. However, what we say must line up with what we heard, what we saw, and what we believe in order to receive it. Find the supporting scripture in the Word of God to pray what you say. Concluding this phase leads to the final stage -- Receive it.

Chapter 7
RECEIVE IT: ARE WE POSITIONED TO RECEIVE WHAT GOD SAID?

Now Mary just had to wait on God to bring His word to pass. She returned to her home to wait for the gift of the Promise –

> *Mary stayed with Elizabeth for three months and then went back to her own home.*
> *Luke 1:56*

Jesus. It was just a matter of God's timing; and as we know, it came to pass (Luke 2). She received the Promise spoken in her hearing and we are receivers of that Gift today.

This reminds me of a pregnant dream I had a few years ago. I was in a labor and delivery room, obviously to give birth, except no one was doing anything. There was a doctor and nurse in the room, but they didn't seem to be in a hurry to prep me. They said I was not ready. In other words, what typically happens before a baby is ready to crown had not happened. My water had not broken, and I had not dilated enough (or not at all).

Maybe that was the case in the natural, but I certainly felt that it was time. Otherwise, I would not have been in labor and delivery. I prepped myself while the medical staff totally ignored my actions. They just stood there, talking to each other and reviewing charts. I put my feet in the stirrups, hoping they would get in position for the delivery; but still, no assistance from either of them. They simply were not moved by what I was doing.

So I got out of the bed, went by a window, and starting praying intensely in the Spirit. I saw them peek up from under their glasses from charts as if thinking, "She has really lost her mind." They looked at each other like I was 'touched.'

Then suddenly the nurse glanced at the bed. She saw a water spot on the sheets. She said, *"Oh my goodness. Your water did break. Get back in the bed!"* Only then they quickly got in position. They could not perceive the spiritual evidence, but they saw the evidence of readiness in the natural. I casually walked back over to the bed and said, "I told you so." Thank God I had already prepped myself!

There will be people in our lives who will not be able to believe like we do because they didn't have the visitation that changed our vision. Therefore, they can't say it in agreement with us. Neither can they help us get in position to receive it. Like Doubting Thomas (John 20:24-29), some will have to actually see an inkling of evidence before they will believe any of it. Therefore, we might just have to war in prayer for it to birth forth which includes the preparation needed for our due season. But before we could even get to this stage of receiving it, we have to go through the other steps: hear it, see it, believe it, and say it.

Not only did Mary hear it, she submitted to God's plan, privileged to be His handmaiden. Any pre-conceived thoughts of her past were replaced with God's plan for her life. God's plan germinated in her mind, and she mentally saw its manifestation. This acceptance then progressed to her heart because she believed it. Then she praised God by saying it, after which it was a matter of waiting for the manifestation to materialize. It came to pass, just as God promised. Mary went from being a virgin woman to the one who gave birth to Jesus, the Christ. She went through the process of being a poor unknown Hebrew girl to become the most honored woman in the history of the world.

| Hear | ⇨ | See | ⇨ | Believe | ⇨ | Say | ⇨ | Receive |

Chapter 8
CONCLUSION

In case you somehow missed how this relates to us, I'll pose these questions:

- Has God spoken something into your hearing that you think is impossible?
- Has God spoken something into your hearing that you think you're too old (or too young) to accomplish?
- Is there something you are passionate about but doubt whether it is achievable?
- Have you aborted a God-given dream to birth something else? If so, why?
- Have you birthed something already, and you're now acknowledging, "*I don't know how to raise and nurture this 'baby'*?
- Did you have a pre-mature delivery, birthing a dream too soon, and now you're not sure how to develop it?
- Do you have a problem believing a God-spoken promise?

Children seem to learn the meaning of the word *'promise'* at an early age. I discovered this from my own son. If I promised to reward him for something, or do something just because I was being a mom, he remembered. So when that time came, guess what? It was time to deliver. I was reminded of my promise; and to him, a promise was a promise! If I didn't fulfill the promise, he would look at me with tear-filled eyes and say, "But you promised." It wasn't in a disrespectful way. He just understood the power in the words, "I promise."

Those missed promises caused me to be more careful using the word *"promise"* because if I promised, he expected mom to deliver! It didn't matter how tired I was or if there was a lack of resources. He had no understanding of those restrictions at that age. He was going on a trusted relationship between mom and son. If I said it, I had to deliver. Why? Because I promised!

Broken promises bring disappointment. Broken promises bring loss of trust. Broken promises cause the word "promise" to be meaningless. It becomes meaningless not just to one, but to others.

I'm so glad that God does not have a problem keeping His promises with us, but sometimes we have a problem hearing, seeing, and believing them so we can say it and receive it. We have a problem co-laboring with God to birth "the baby" so we just remain in a spiritual blind state.

This realization takes me back to my grandmother dream shared in the first chapter. Therefore, I believe the image of my grandmother represents many of us in the Body of Christ for many reasons, including the following scenarios:

- We heard the Word spoken but we're having difficulty seeing it; therefore, we remain spiritually blind and continue to function in our current state.
- We didn't hear it because we were not in the right position (or quiet enough) to hear so we continue to function in a state of what we think is normal.

- Our situation, tradition, or others (the nay-sayers) tell us things will never change so we believe the lie without even trying.
- We tried to believe before but the steps forward were just too hard so we stopped and shelved the vision (or threw it away).

Regardless of our reason, the reality is that nothing will change until we hear the door bell ringing and open the door for the Deliver to come in! Once He's in, we must be willing to allow Him access to all areas in order to bring change to our situation and others we are *infecting and affecting*. In other words, make a decision. That's the starting point. Then seek Him for the plan and timing, and move on it.

Sunday after Sunday, message after message, prophecy after prophecy, we hear them all. We get excited for a moment; however, unless that fire is kept ablaze inside by the Holy Spirit, we can easily revert back to just functioning. I believe God is ready to blow upon our embers and set a fire within us so we can move forward.

Therefore, we need to take a moment of solitude to hear what the Lord (our Deliverer) has to say. We need Him to show us another way to get untangled or unstuck so we can move forward. But just like Mary, we have to be positioned in relationship with God to hear the message from our Messenger, have the vision to see what is being spoken (even the impossible), get it in our hearts so we can believe it, begin to say it out of our mouths in agreement, and then wait for the manifestation so we can receive it. It's just that simple on one hand; but do not be disillusioned. It may not necessarily be a "cake walk" to fulfillment. Just like Mary, you may have to forfeit your comforts for the uncomfortable.

We have heard this mantra many times, and it is worth repeating here. God never promised us a bed of ease, but He promised, if we follow Him, we'll never have to walk alone.

If my grandmother had heard the message from the Messenger (the Deliverer), who obviously had been there before, perhaps she would have sought the help and received it. She would not have been operating in spiritual blindness, and neither would the host of generations seated at the dinner table. I believe this is a part of passing on generation blessings.

I believe there are generational blessings that come with freedom from just one taking a step! If she believed there would be a fulfillment of those things the Lord (the Deliverer) told her (Luke 1:45), it would have taken her from a limited way of thinking to thinking like a limitless God.

According to Psalm 37:4, *Delight yourself also in the Lord, and He shall give you the desires of your heart:* what's in our heart should be His heart. For years, I read this scripture without the full understanding until revealed by the Holy Spirit. Perhaps you and others thought like I did previously.

Earlier in my walk, I thought it meant that, as long as I was trying to live right, trying to do the right thing, and not asking for "sinful" things, He would give me the desires of my heart. Never did I imagine that I get my desires when His desires become my desires. It's then that I have a heart change to the things of God. It's then that I have a transformed mind. What a powerful scripture!

It's a God transplanted heart! When we make God's delight our delight, we get them. To receive what He wants us to have, we've got to hear Him and remove our spiritual blinders so we can see it, thereby getting it in our heart to believe it. His word will not return to Him void (Isaiah 55:10-11). However, we have an obligation to fulfill. We must cooperate. Only then will more transforming work begin.

To receive the promises requires that we die to our flesh. I call it the "flesh death." It's letting go of the things we thought were important in exchange for what God says is truly important. It's allowing God to drive our car!

I am reminded of a vision God gave me several years ago while praying. I asked God to take control of a situation, but I was still in the drivers' seat. In the vision, half of my hip was in the seat with one hand still on the steering wheel, not fully relinquishing control to God. I even patted the other half of the seat as if to say, *"You can sit right here. See, I made room for You."* Imagine that! As if I was doing God a favor. I'm so glad God has a sense of humor. He has to in order to deal with each of us and our personalities.

Removal of spiritual blinders requires change. If we're going to change, we must go through the change process which comes through a relationship with God, our Father, through Jesus Christ. His Word will come to life in every area of our lives. If we want to see, we have to go through the process as orchestrated by God, our Deliverer.

Just quoting scripture will not get us there. *"Be not conformed to this world but be ye transformed by the renewing of our mind."* In Romans 12:2, we must be willing to be transformed. We can't just know about Corinthians 13, often referred to as the love chapter; we've got to make sure we love by doing it. Flesh death is a total surrender to the Spirit of God. He kills my flesh very softly and gently with

His word; forever changing my entire life by His word. His word is sharp (Hebrews 4:12).

God is moving in ways like never before, and there is no room for grey areas in our lives. Either we're in or we're out. Either we will or we won't. Either we're hot or we're cold. However, the price that we pay (the consequences) for operating in our free will are too high. We can no longer afford to conform to the worldly way of doing things. We must transform our mind so that our hearts will be changed. Then our mouths will line up with what we believe in our heart. That's the way we receive His spoken promises.

As the Body of Christ, we cannot keep doing things the same way and expect new results. God is doing a new thing. *"Behold, I will do a new thing, now it shall spring forth; Shall you not know it? I will even make a road in the wilderness and rivers in the desert." Isaiah 43:9.*

Without vision, we perish. Just like Mary, we need to follow the steps. Then at the right time, get in the stirrups and push when He says push. Yes, there are spiritual births happening; but just like with a natural birth, the baby in the womb must be nurtured properly until developed and ready to be birthed. The same is true for spiritual births, too. We have to care for the seeds God impregnates within us until it's time for them to come forth.

If there is one thing I know about seeds it's this: that everything needed to produce the product is already in the seed. It doesn't matter how large or small the seed is, it's all included. It just needs to be in the right ground (the soil of our heart), along with the proper nourishment (the Word of God) as it grows, then the harvest comes. In other words, seed-time-harvest!

In the dream, my grandmother settled for the mediocre way of living due to her spiritual blindness. It limited her. Even after the Deliverer showed up, she still could not "see" Him. But this time, there was at least one who heard the bell ringing and responded. Not just to fix something, but to fix generations.

Many of us have our shelves lined with various books on God's promises. We can quote almost every scripture accurately and eloquently. However, if we're not hearing God for ourselves and grabbing hold of the vision as He reveals them, then we will never be able to get it in our heart to be able to quote what He says and receive it. If we don't, we will miss our divine appointments and will be unable to connect to our next one. As the ripple effect goes, sadly enough, our spiritual blindness may cause others connected to us to miss their spiritual connection, too.

I'll leave you with this final thought: Just like Mary's visitation changed her life, in the grandmother dream, a visitation from the Deliverer can change our lives if we are willing. The Repairman responded to a call to fix something perceived to be broken, but it really was a bigger fix than originally anticipated. It could have been in response to the cries and prayers of intercession from days gone by for the family or a situation.

Instead of my grandmother saying, "I've been meaning to go to the doctor but ...", and fill in any excuse we want, the Physician (the Deliverer) showed up, responding to a call. He knew the thing He was called to fix was not the real problem. He rang the bell hoping for someone, at least one person, to let Him in and allow Him to heal the things that have been holding generations captive for years. He came so that the head of the house (my grandmother in this case because my grandfather was deceased) could be healed and so could entire generations!

Chapter 9
THE DECISION

The Repairman knows what really needs to be fixed inside "the house". Therefore, if we respond positively, good things happen. We are the keepers of our doors. Those who hear and respond by opening the door and cooperating with the Repairman (the Deliverer) will be fixed. The other choice is to continue in dysfunctional behavior.

Is Jesus, the Deliverer, knocking at our door to deal with a situation? Are we in position to hear and respond properly? Are we ready to go through the change process so He can take us other places? Are we ready for His light to come into our darkness?

The last time I saw the Repairman in the dream, He confirmed what I saw and kept walking through the house. I would imagine if Grandma had responded to my original question, admitting the truth and agreed to the help from the Visitor, perhaps the scene at the dinner table would have been different.

If you are tired of just functioning based on old ideas or if you are tired of walking in spiritual blindness, today is your day. Because Mary was obedient, she heard, saw, believed, said, and received the Promise. Those who have a relationship with God through Jesus Christ have this same access of receiving. We just have to put the process to work and acknowledge areas in need of correction, direction, deflection, you name it.

However, for those who do not have a relationship with God through Jesus Christ, His Son, you can do so today. It's simple. The Word says in Romans 10:9, *that if you confess with your mouth the Lord Jesus and believe in your heart that God has raised Him from the dead, you will be saved.* Therefore, you can simply say:

> Lord, according to Romans 10:9, You said that if we confess the Lord Jesus and believe in our hearts that God raised Jesus from the dead, we shall be saved. So right now, I confess that Jesus is Lord. I believe in my heart that God raised Jesus from the dead. I accept Jesus Christ as my personal Savior and according to Your word, I am now saved.

If you just prayed this simple prayer you're saved. I encourage you to allow the Lord to lead you to a Body of Believers where you can grow in your relationship with Him so your roots can grow deep (Psalm 1:1-3).

Now you too will begin to hear, see, believe, say, and receive because you will have access to the Promise -- the one and only Savior, Jesus Christ. You may not get everything you want (notice I said "you want") but one thing is for sure -- you'll get what you need!

May God bless you all on your journey of hearing, seeing, believing, saying, and receiving!

It's Your Turn

Hear ⇨ See ⇨ Believe ⇨ Say ⇨ Receive

Hear: What did God say?

See: What do you see?

Believe: What's in your heart?

Say: What are you speaking? What scriptures are you standing on?

Receive: Are you prepared and in position to receive?

About the Author

Karen Seymore Portman is a highly sought-after mentor, coach, seminar presenter, and teacher, and handles it all with humility. It only takes one encounter with Karen to realize she is gifted and anointed to do the work God has assigned to her hands. Her unquenchable desire to serve and her boundless energy makes her a formidable talent to harness. She equips equippers.

She plants intercessory prayer ministries; conducts various workshops on emotional healing, vision and purpose, prayer, women's issues, and a variety of other topics; teaches all generations; assists with revivals; and teaches all levels of prophetic classes for a virtual global school.

Karen operates in many spiritual gifts, teaching is but one of them. Her creativity in teaching classes is cleaver, vibrant, and delightful. The mark of a great teacher is that students seek them. She employs an unusual teaching style of first teaching a basic concept then immediately requiring students to demonstrate how the information is applied.

With a deep compassion to see people saved and fulfilling their destiny promised by God, Karen is driven to reach the lost, minister to individuals, and encourage people of all ages to walk in their purpose created by God.

This explains her call scripture in 2004, Isaiah 61:1-3 – *'to preach the gospel and to heal the brokenhearted'*. Although that's just one of her many favorite scriptures, as she continues to avail herself to the Lord, the one that could best represent her is found in Isaiah 6:8 -- ***Also I heard the voice of the Lord, saying: " Whom shall I send, and who will go for Us?" Then I said, "Here am I! Send me."***